Introduction

$\mathcal{B}$lending 18th century flavor with 20th century tastes, historic New Orleans is a mecca of luscious food born in the Louisiana bottom lands and evolved from the merging of local ingredients by multicultural settlers into culinary creations unique throughout the world. The unusual confluence of salt water sea and steaming swamps, of lagoons and low lying land, of misty marshes and bayous near the mouth of the mighty Mississippi River, provide a distinctive pantry from which generations of home cooks and restaurant chefs have innovated bold and sensational cooking that is sophisticated yet simple.

Early settlers discovered a wealth of resources from land and sea. Oysters, crabs, shrimp, lobster, crawfish and frogs filled the local tidewaters, along with an abundance of fresh water and salt water fish. Rice and sugar cane thrived in the wet lands; onions, okra, tomatoes, squash, potatoes, yams and fruits flourished on fertile inland soils.

The French pioneers, the Cajuns, brought their cooking techniques and love of fine food to this bountiful region. Native American Indians introduced the use of filé, a powder of ground dried sassafras leaves, in gumbos; and contributed methods for preparing corn and wild game. Spanish and Italian settlers furnished their favorite spices and sauces. Descendants of the early French settlers became known as Creoles. Africans and West Indians added a Caribbean influence to this myriad melting pot, all of which combined to create celebrated Creole cooking.

Strollers through the picturesque French Quarter, the city's earliest settlement, as well as travelers through the beautiful Garden District, enjoy a sensory deluge as they experience exotic odors from the kitchens of some of the world's finest restaurants...cooking smells so intoxicating as to linger forever on the palate of one's memory. The classic recipes in this Keepsake Collection are basic and easy. You can relive the culinary pleasures of Louisiana's fabulous foods and savor the flavors of fine family or company fare at your own table at home.

© **Keepsake Cuisine Series**

Appetizers

Oysters
Rockefeller

Crab
Canapés

Clams
Casino

Oysters
on the Half
Shell

And other
favorites

Oysters on the Half Shell

Clams Casino

12 -24 clams, depending on size
1/4 cup butter at room temperature
1 tablespoon finely minced pimiento
1 tablespoon finely minced green pepper
1 tablespoon finely minced celery
1/4 cup fine bread crumbs
1 teaspoon anchovy paste
6 slices bacon

Heat oven to 425 degrees. Scrub clams thoroughly and open with a strong knife. Cut clam away from shell but leave in half shell. Combine butter, pimiento, green pepper, celery, bread crumbs and anchovy paste. Work mixture to a paste and spread onto opened clams. Cut bacon into pieces large enough to cover each clam and place on top of mixture. Bake 8 to 10 minutes or until bacon is done.

Oysters on the Half Shell

6 fresh shucked oysters per serving
   Lemon wedges
   Hot pepper sauce
   Ground black pepper
   Buttered toast points

To shuck oysters, insert strong knife into hinge side of shell and twist to open. Loosen each oyster from the deeper half shell but let it remain in the shell. Discard other half. Serve on a bed of cracked ice around a small bowl of hot pepper sauce. Sprinkle with coarse ground black pepper and a squeeze of lemon. Serve with toast points.

Oysters Rockefeller

Oysters Rockefeller

Rock salt
12　medium oysters in shell
1/4　cup butter
2　tablespoons onion, finely chopped
2　tablespoons celery, finely chopped
2　tablespoons snipped parsley
1/2　cup fresh spinach, chopped small
1/3　cup dry bread crumbs, divided
1/3　cup Parmesan cheese
　　Salt and pepper
　　Few drops of hot pepper sauce and
　　Worcestershire Sauce and Anchovy Paste

Preheat oven to 450 degrees. Fill two 9" glass pie pans, or other oven-proof serving platters, with 1/2" rock salt. Prepare oysters for half shell as directed on page 3. Arrange filled shells on rock salt base. Melt butter in skillet and sauté onion, celery and parsley until onion is tender. Mix in remaining ingredients, except one half of bread crumbs and Parmesan cheese. Spoon about 1 tablespoon spinach mixture onto oyster in each shell. Sprinkle with remaining bread crumbs and Parmesan cheese. Bake until heated through, about 10 minutes. Serves 2.

Chicken Liver Pâté

1　cup (2 sticks) butter
1　pound chicken livers
1　small onion, chopped
1/2　teaspoon curry powder
1/2　teaspoon paprika
1/8　teaspoon salt
　　Pinch of pepper
2　teaspoons brandy

Melt 4 tablespoons of butter in a skillet. Add livers, onions, curry powder, paprika, salt and pepper. Cover and cook for 5 minutes or until livers are firm but still pink inside. Cool mixture slightly; put into electric blender. Whirl until smooth, stopping blender to scrape sides of container often. Add remaining butter and brandy. Pack into a small bowl or crock. Chill. Serve with toast or crackers. Makes 2 cups.

Crab Meat Canapés

1　cup fresh lump crab meat, picked over
　　well to remove any shell bits
1/4　cup mayonnaise
1　tablespoon chopped parsley
1　tablespoon chopped chives
1　teaspoon lemon juice
1　teaspoon Worcestershire sauce
　　hot pepper sauce to taste
　　Freshly ground pepper to taste
　　Toast rounds

French Quarter Balconies

Combine the crab meat with the mayonnaise, herbs and seasonings. Spread on rounds of toast. Broil until browned. Makes 16 canapés.

Shrimp Cocktail

6   **large cooked shrimp, per serving, deveined**
      with tails on
      Lemon wedges

1   **cup catsup**
2   **tablespoons horseradish**
1   **tablespoon lemon juice**
1   **tablespoon tarragon vinegar**
1   **tablespoon Worcestershire**
      Dash of hot pepper sauce
      Salt and garlic salt to taste

Combine all ingredients except shrimp and lemon wedges and chill thoroughly. Mix shrimp with sauce and serve in lettuce-lined cocktail sherbet glasses with a wedge of lemon for each.

Oysters en Brochette

2   **dozen raw oysters**
4   **eight-inch skewers**
12   **strips bacon, cut in half**
1   **egg**
3/4   **cup milk**
      Salt and pepper to taste
1/2   **flour**
      Oil for frying
      Lemon wedge

Fry bacon until not quite crisp. Alternate six oysters and six half strips of bacon (folded) on each skewer. Make a batter with egg and milk and season well with salt and pepper. Dip each skewer in batter, roll in flour and deep fry until golden. Serve on toast points with lemon wedge. Serves 4 as appetizer or 2 as main course.

Soups & Salads

Carrot Salad

❦

Tomato Cucumber Salad

❦

Clam Chowder

❦

Oyster Stew

❦

And other favorites

Oyster Stew

Creole Coleslaw

2	medium heads cabbage, shredded
1/2	cup mayonnaise
2	tablespoons white vinegar
1	tablespoon sugar
3	large carrots, peeled and shredded
1/2	bunch green onions, chopped
1/2	cup sour cream
2	tablespoons yellow mustard
	Salt and white pepper to taste

Mix all ingredients and chill. Serves 6.

Coleslaw Dressing

1/2	cup cider vinegar
1½	teaspoons dry mustard
4	eggs
2	cups light cream
	Dash of salt
¼-½	cup sugar
2	tablespoons butter

Combine the vinegar and mustard in the top of a double boiler and let stand ten minutes. Beat the eggs lightly and add them to the vinegar. Add the cream, salt and sugar and cook, stirring with a wooden spoon, until the mixture coats the spoon. Remove the sauce from the heat and swirl in the butter. Makes 3 cups.

Oyster Stew

3	dozen oysters with liquid
2	tablespoons butter
1	tablespoon flour
2	tablespoons chopped green onions
2	cups half and half (milk/cream)
1	teaspoon butter
1/4	teaspoon salt
1	dash hot pepper sauce

Heat oysters in liquid until their edges curl, then set aside to keep warm. Melt butter in a saucepan, blend in flour until smooth, stir in chopped green onions and simmer a few minutes. Pour into a blender with oyster liquid and one dozen of the oysters. Blend first on low, then high for about a minute. While blending, add cream (at room temperature). Melt one teaspoon of butter in a double boiler, add oyster mixture and stir until well heated and thickened. Season to taste. Add remaining oysters, or place six oysters in each warmed soup bowl and pour stew over them. Garnish with paprika. Serves 4.

French Quarter

Cream of Vegetable Soup

3	tablespoons butter
2-3	medium onions, chopped
3	tablespoons flour
1½	teaspoons salt
	Dash of pepper
3	cups milk
	Vegetable pulp and cooking liquid, about 2 cups (*recipe follows*)
1/3	cup cream (optional)

Heat butter; add onion and simmer five minutes until soft but not browned. Stir in flour and seasonings; remove from heat and slowly add milk; stirring until well blended; return to low heat and cook until thick and smooth, stirring constantly. Add vegetable pulp and liquid. Reheat before serving, adding cream if desired. Garnish each serving with chopped parsley, chives or water cress or a dash of paprika. Serves 6.

Vegetable Pulp
Vegetable Options

2 pounds asparagus in 1" lengths cooked until tender in 1-1/2 cups chicken broth or water; *or*

3 cups shredded carrots cooked in 1-1/2 cups chicken broth or water about 10 minutes; *or*

2 cups diced celery cooked covered in 1 cup of milk in top of double boiler until tender; *or*

1 pound fresh spinach cooked covered in water which clings to leaves.

Place cooked vegetables into a blender and purée until smooth. Measure pulp and add cooking liquid or milk to make 2 cups. Add pulp to cream soup as directed.

Tomato Cucumber Salad

3   ripe tomatoes
1   large cucumber
1   large red onion

Slice vegetables evenly and arrange in alternate layers on plate. Drizzle with vinaigrette and shredded fresh basil. Serve immediately. Serves 6.

Vinaigrette:
1/4   cup extra virgin olive oil
3   tablespoons red wine vinegar
1   teaspoon Dijon mustard
     Salt and pepper to taste

Whisk together until thoroughly mixed.

Carrot Walnut Salad

3   large carrots, shredded
1   tablespoon extra virgin olive oil
2   teaspoons fresh lemon juice
1/4   teaspoon salt
$1\frac{1}{2}$ tablespoons walnuts, chopped and lightly toasted

Toss carrots with oil in bowl. Add remaining ingredients and toss well. Serves 2.

Carrot Walnut Salad

Mardi Gras Salad

1   can petite green peas
1   can French style green beans
$1\frac{1}{2}$ cups diced celery
1   diced green pepper
1   small jar chopped pimiento
1   small onion, diced
1/2   cup sugar
1/2   cup vegetable oil
1   tablespoon salt
1/3   cup vinegar

Drain juices from peas, beans and pimiento. Mix all ingredients in mixing bowl. Cover and marinate in refrigerator for 12 hours. Serves 4.

Ambrosia

2   large oranges
2   medium bananas
1   medium pineapple, cored and cubed *or*
     1 twenty ounce can pineapple chunks
1/2   cup shredded coconut
     Mint sprigs to garnish

Peel and segment oranges. Slice bananas and combine with pineapple and coconut. Chill and serve. Garnish with fresh mint. Serves 6.

Tomato & Cucumber Salad

Clam Chowder

Clam Chowder

2	pounds clams (1 lb. shelled or canned clams)
3	oz. rindless bacon, diced
1	medium onion, finely diced
1	tablespoon flour
6	medium potatoes, peeled and cubed
4	cups milk
1	cup light cream
	Chopped parsley (optional)

Sauté bacon until fat is rendered. Remove bacon and set aside. Add onions to pan and cook until softened. Add the potatoes, salt, pepper, milk and reserved clam juice. Cover and boil twelve minutes or until potatoes are tender. Add the clams, cream, parsley and bacon and heat through. Do not boil. Serves 6.

Potato Salad

2	cups cooked potatoes, diced
1/2	cup diced cucumber
1	tablespoon minced onion
1/2	cup celery, diced
3/4	teaspoon celery seed
1$\frac{1}{2}$	teaspoon salt
1/2	teaspoon pepper
3	hard cooked eggs
1	cup sour cream
1/2	cup mayonnaise or salad dressing
1/4	cup vinegar
1	teaspoon prepared mustard

Lightly toss potatoes, cucumber, onion, celery, celery seed, salt and pepper. Separate yolks from whites of eggs. Dice whites and add to potato mixture. Mash yolks and combine with sour cream, mayonnaise, vinegar and mustard. Add to potatoes and toss together lightly. Chill. Garnish with crisp salad greens. Serves 8.

Vegetables & Side Dishes

Stuffed Artichokes

Dirty Rice

Onion Cheese Pie

Red Beans & Rice

And other favorites

Red Beans & Rice

Red Beans & Rice

Typical Louisiana food, the South's equivalent of Italian spaghetti dishes, and just as good.

2   cups (1 pound) dried red kidney beans
5   strips bacon or 1/4 pound salt pork or ham bone
1/2 cup uncooked rice
2½ quarts water
1   clove garlic
    Salt and pepper to taste

Soak beans overnight in one quart of water in a heavy pot. Drain. Add another one and one half quarts of water, cut up bacon (or ham bone or salt pork), garlic and a little salt. Simmer slowly three or four hours until beans are very soft and water has cooked down to a thick red sauce. Add salt and pepper to taste and serve over cooked hot, fluffy rice. Serves 6. (Left-over beans can be made into soup by puréeing in the blender with some chicken bouillon and a little lemon juice. Stir in one tablespoon sherry per serving and sprinkle hard boiled egg on top.)

Twice Baked Potato

1   large baking potato per serving
2   teaspoons butter
1   heaping teaspoon chopped chives
    Salt and pepper to taste
3   heaping teaspoons sour cream
3   heaping teaspoons grated sharp Cheddar cheese

Bake potato about 40 minutes at 375 degrees until soft. Cut a cross in the top of each potato so that steam can escape. Break potato away from skin with a fork, being careful not to scoop out of potato. Add butter, salt and pepper. Mix into potato. Add sour cream, chives and grated cheese. Stir and mix carefully so as not to break the potato skin. Sprinkle with additional cheese. Bake for 15 minutes or until cheese melts and begin to brown at edges.

Sweet Potato Casserole

2	cups cooked mashed sweet potatoes
1/2	cup brown sugar
1	teaspoon cinnamon
1	teaspoon vanilla
1/8	teaspoon salt
2	large eggs
1	can (12 oz.) evaporated milk
20	marshmallows

Beat together first six ingredients with mixer at medium speed. Beat in milk gradually. Pour into a 9 inch square baking dish. Bake at 375 degrees about 35 minutes or until knife inserted in center comes out clean. Remove from oven. Top with marshmallows and return to oven for about 12 minutes, or until marshmallows are puffed and browned. Serves 6.

Stuffed Baked Eggplant

2	firm eggplants
4	tablespoons shallots, finely chopped
1	tablespoon chopped parsley
1	stick butter
1	cup cooked shrimp
1	cup lump crab meat
	Salt and pepper to taste
1	cup Parmesan cheese, finely grated
1/4	cup bread crumbs

Cut eggplants in half and place in the oven at 375 degrees in a pan with a cup of water in the bottom to steam the eggplant. Cook until tender, about thirty minutes. Carefully remove the pulp with a spoon so that you do not break the skin. Brown shallots and parsley in butter over low heat. Add shrimp, crab meat and the eggplant pulp. Season with salt and pepper. Stir together and cook for five minutes. Fill the shells. Sprinkle cheese and bread crumbs over the top of each eggplant. Bake at 350 degrees until tops are browned. Serves 4.

Dirty Rice

	Chicken gizzards, necks, livers and hearts (approx. 1 pound total)
2	pounds hot sausage
1/2	cup ham, diced
1	large yellow onion, minced
2	ribs celery, finely chopped
1	small bell pepper, finely chopped
1/2	bunch green onions, minced
4	tablespoons butter
1	tablespoon dried parsley
	Salt to taste
4-6	cups cooked rice

Boil gizzards, necks, livers and hearts in two quarts of water until done. Save water. Fry hot sausage and render grease. Simmer yellow onions, celery and pepper in 3 tablespoons sausage grease for 20 minutes. Add green onions and simmer for 10 minutes more. Combine chopped chicken, sausage and ham with sautéed vegetables and stir in butter and parsley. Add salt to taste and some of the saved water. Simmer for 15 minutes more, then fold in rice. Hold in double boiler to keep warm. Serves 12.

Rice is believed to have been brought to the United States in the late 1600's when a ship from Madagascar, damaged by storms, took refuge in the Charleston, South Carolina harbor. The ship's captain presented the governor with a sack of seed rice. South Carolina became the leading rice producer in the U.S. until 1889, when Louisiana claimed the lead, later sharing the distinction with California and Texas.

Stuffed Artichoke

Eggplant and Tomato Casserole

1/4 cup salad oil

1   medium onion, chopped

3/4 cup mushrooms, sliced

1/2 medium green pepper, chopped

1   medium eggplant, cut into one inch cubes, peeled

1   16 ounce can plum tomatoes

1   teaspoon salt

1   tablespoon chopped parsley

2   eggs, beaten

1   cup Parmesan cheese, finely grated

1   cup Mozzarella cheese, finely grated

Heat oil in large frying pan and add onions, mushrooms and green pepper. Sauté over medium heat until vegetables are limp, about 2 minutes. Stir in eggplant, tomatoes, salt and parsley. Cover and simmer slowly until eggplant is tender, about 30 minutes, stirring often. Uncover and increase heat, if needed, to reduce liquid. Meanwhile, combine Parmesan and Mozzarella with eggs. Spoon half of eggplant mixture into a 2-1/2 quart casserole and top with half the cheese mixture. Repeat layers, ending with cheese mixture. Bake uncovered in 375 degree oven for 30 minutes. If prepared ahead and dish is cold, bake for 45 minutes. Serves 6.

Corn Pudding

4-6 ears fresh corn

3   beaten eggs

11/2 cup milk

1   teaspoon sugar

     Dash salt

3   tablespoons butter

Cut corn from cobs and scrape ears. Combine all ingredients in buttered 1-1/2 quart casserole. Bake at 350 degrees for 45 minutes, or until set. Serves 6.

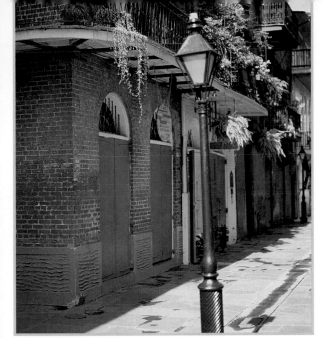

Alley in the French Quarter

Stuffed Artichoke

5	large artichokes
5	cloves garlic, finely cut
1/2	cup bread crumbs
1 1/2	cup saltine crackers
1/2	cup parsley flakes
1/2	cup Parmesan cheese
5	tablespoons olive oil

Snip off pointed ends of artichoke leaves; wash well. Drain upside down. Mix dry ingredients together on waxed paper and roll with rolling pin to make crumbs. Scoop crumb mixture into artichokes, separating leaves as you do. Place in a large pot of shallow salt water, add garlic cloves. Pour olive oil generously over each artichoke. Bring to a boil and simmer about 1 hour. Add more water as necessary. Serves 5.

Green Beans Southern Style

1	pound fresh green beans
4	slices bacon
2	tablespoons shallots or onions, finely chopped

Cook green beans until barely tender. Meanwhile, sauté bacon until crisp. Remove from pan onto paper towel. Crumble. Pour off all but 1 tablespoon fat from pan. Sauté onion or shallots in pan for 3 minutes. Add green beans and bacon. Heat through. Season with salt and pepper. Serves 4.

Onion Cheese Pie

1	crumb crust (recipe follows)
2 1/3	cups Spanish or Vidalia onions, minced
1	tablespoon butter or margarine
3/4	cup (3 ounces) sharp Cheddar cheese, shredded
3	eggs, beaten
1	cup milk
1/2	teaspoon Italian seasoning
	Pinch of salt and pepper
	Onion rings or parsley sprigs (optional)

Sauté chopped onions in one tablespoon butter until tender. Remove from heat. Stir in cheese and spoon into prepared crust. Combine eggs, milk and seasonings. Stir well. Pour over onion cheese mixture. Bake at 375 degrees for 30 minutes or until set. Let stand 10 minutes before serving. Garnish with onion rings and parsley, if desired.

Crumb Crust

2	cups cheese flavored cracker crumbs
1/3	cup butter or margarine

Melt butter and combine with cracker crumbs. Mix well. Press into bottom and up sides of a 9" pie pan. Bake at 350 degrees for 5 minutes. Yields one 9" pie shell.

Green Beans

Cajun

Seafood
Gumbo

Crawfish
Boil

Blackened
Red
Snapper

Jambalaya

And other
favorites

Blackened Red Snapper

Roux (Brown or White)

3   **tablespoons butter or fat**
3   **tablespoons flour**

This is the foundation of all sauces and gravies. The Creole cook, like the French, believes that the success of sauce depends upon its brown or white roux. To make roux, melt the butter or fat slowly and gradually add the flour, stirring constantly until all is a delicate brown. Brown roux must never be overly browned or burned. Other ingredients may be added as the browning continues. The secret of good roux lies in the gradual introduction of ingredients. Continue to stir until roux is a delicate brown and slowly add 1 cup brown stock, consomme or water. When sauce reaches a good consistency, add seasonings as desired. A white roux is made like the brown except that the flour and butter are blended together at the same time and not allowed to brown. This roux is used for sauces containing milk or cream.

Blackened Red Snapper

    Red Snapper fillets
    For each serving, prepare:
1/3   **teaspoon garlic powder**
2/3   **teaspoon onion powder**
1/3   **teaspoon cayenne**
2/3   **teaspoon paprika**
1/2   **teaspoon salt**
1/4   **teaspoon pepper**
1/3   **teaspoon dried thyme**
    Dash ground cumin

Dredge fish in above spice mixture. Drizzle with melted butter and sauté in a very hot, heavy (cast iron) skillet until blackened, only a few minutes per side. Turn and repeat on other side.

Shrimp Jambalaya

Seafood Gumbo

1/4	cup flour
8	small white onions, peeled
7	tablespoons butter
2	8 ounce bottles clam juice
1	16 ounce can plum tomatoes, drained
1	bay leaf
1	teaspoon Worcestershire sauce
	Dash of salt
1/4	teaspoon thyme
1/2	teaspoon sugar
	Dash of ground pepper
2	pounds shrimp, cooked, shelled and, deveined or 2 pounds lump crab meat or cleaned crayfish or a combination
1	package frozen okra
1	green pepper, seeded and cut in strips
2	ribs celery, trimmed and cut into 1/2" pieces
	Parsley sprigs, chopped

Preheat oven to 350 degrees. Place the flour on aluminum foil and bake, stirring occasionally, until hazelnut brown, about 10 minutes. Combine onions and 4 tablespoons of the butter in a saucepan. Toss briefly. Cover and cook until onions become translucent, about 5 minutes. Sprinkle the onions with the browned flour. Stir in clam juice with a wire whisk. Continue stirring until mixture is thickened and smooth. Add the tomatoes, bay leaf, Worcestershire, seasonings and sugar. Add the shrimp and cook 10 minutes. Add the okra and cook, stirring, until pieces of the okra separate. Cook the green pepper and celery in the remaining butter about 3 minutes, stirring. The vegetables must remain crisp. Add the vegetables to the onion mixture and cook 10 to 15 minutes longer, or until celery is tender but still somewhat crisp. Sprinkle with chopped parsley and serve. Serves 6.

Shrimp Jambalaya

1/4	cup cooking oil
1/2	pound smoked sausage, sliced
1/2	pound ham, cubed
1	cup onions, chopped
1	cup bell pepper, chopped
1	cup celery, chopped
1	cup green onions, chopped
2	cloves garlic, minced
1	16 ounce can tomatoes, drained, reserving liquid
1	teaspoon thyme
1	teaspoon black pepper
1/4	teaspoon cayenne pepper
1	teaspoon salt
1	cup converted rice
1½	cups stock or water
1½	tablespoons Worcestershire sauce
2	pounds peeled shrimp

Sauté sausage and ham in a heavy Dutch oven until slightly browned. Remove from pot. Sauté onions, bell peppers, celery, green onions and garlic in meat drippings until tender. Add tomatoes, thyme, pepper and salt. Cook for five minutes. Stir in rice. Mix together liquid from tomatoes, stock and Worcestershire sauce to equal 2-1/2 cups. Bring to a boil, reduce to simmer, add raw shrimp, ham and sausage and cook uncovered, stirring occasionally for about 30 minutes or until rice and shrimp are done. Serves 12.

Blackened Chicken Salad

2	medium boneless chicken breast halves
2	tablespoons butter
1/3	teaspoon garlic powder
2/3	teaspoon onion powder
1/3	teaspoon cayenne
2/3	teaspoon paprika
1/2	teaspoon salt
1/4	teaspoon pepper
1/3	teaspoon dried thyme
	Dash of ground cumin

Melt the butter. Dip chicken in butter and dredge into mixture of all the spices. Heat a heavy skillet to high heat. Drizzle a teaspoon of the butter onto the seasoned chicken and sauté several at a time, butter side down, until blackened. Turn and repeat. Arrange the sliced chicken on a bed of mixed greens and serve with honey-mustard dressing.

Honey-Mustard Dressing

1/2	cup vegetable oil
1/3	cup honey
1/4	cup lemon juice
1	tablespoon Dijon mustard

Shake all ingredients in tightly covered container. Shake before serving. Makes one cup.

Blackened Chicken Salad

Filé Gumbo

Chicken Jambalaya

9   chicken thighs

1   pound smoked sausage

1/4 cup light olive oil, divided

3   medium onions

4   ribs celery

5   cloves garlic

2   bell peppers

1   8 ounce can tomato paste

1   16 ounce can tomatoes

    Dash cayenne pepper

    Dash of chili powder

    Dash of parsley flakes

1   tablespoon Worcestershire sauce

1/2 teaspoon hot pepper sauce

    Salt and pepper to taste

1   cup rice

3   bay leaves

In a large skillet, brown chicken and sausage quickly in 2 tablespoons olive oil, then add water and poach until tender. Reserve liquid. Sauté chopped onion, celery, garlic and bell peppers in remaining olive oil. Add cut up chicken and sausage, tomatoes and tomato paste. Stir in seasonings to taste. Cook for 40 minutes on low heat. Add rice along with 2-1/2 cups of reserved liquid. Cook covered until rice is tender. Serves 8.

Filé Gumbo

1   bunch green onions, chopped

2   tablespoons bacon fat

3   tablespoons flour

1   sprig parsley, chopped

1/2 teaspoon thyme

1   stalk celery, chopped

2   cups oyster liquid

4   cups water

1   pound raw shrimp, or crawfish, shelled

    Salt, pepper and cayenne to taste

2   dozen oysters

1/2 teaspoon filé powder

Sauté onions in fat in a deep heavy pot. Stir in flour and add chopped parsley, thyme and celery. Cook for a few minutes and add oyster liquid and water, shrimp and seasoning. Cover and cook slowly for l-1/2 hours. Add oysters and cook until their edges curl. Remove from heat and stir in file powder. Gumbo should never be cooked after filé is added as it will become too thick. If you prepare in advance, do not add filé until final heating. Serve in soup bowls with hot fluffy rice. Serves 6.

Rather than discard left over rice water, use it as a spray starch for ironing cottons and linens.

Strolling near Jackson Square

Crawfish Boil

1   carrot, sliced in rounds

1   large onion, sliced

2   shallots or scallions, including green part, coarsely chopped

2   cups water

2   cups dry white wine

     Salt to taste

12   peppercorns

2   sprigs parsley

1   bay leaf

     Pinch of thyme

4-6   dozen crawfish

     Parsley for garnish

Combine carrot, onion, shallots or scallions, water, wine, salt, peppercorns, two sprigs parsley, bay leaf and thyme in a kettle and bring to a boil. Reduce heat and simmer 15 minutes. Wash the crawfish well and drop them into the courtbouillon. Return to a boil and remove from heat. Let the crawfish cool in the liquid. Drain and arrange in a pile with parsley for garnish. Serve with a dipping sauce and eat with the fingers. Serves 4.

For perfect rice, the cook should set the heat so low as to take up to fifteen minutes for the rice and water to come to a boil, then take up a grain and chew it. If there is a hard spot left in the middle of the grain, the rice is not done. Continue tasting every minute or so until cooked through. Pour off most of the water, pour rice into colander and rinse with cold water, then set colander over a tall pot in which there are a few inches of slowing boiling water, and allow to steam for half an hour. Never steam rice in a low pot. If the steaming water touches the rice, it will become soggy and not be fit to eat. This method never fails to give a delicious dish of rice with every grain separate.

Seafood

Fried Catfish

❧

Crab Cakes

❧

Trout Amandine

❧

Shrimp Creole

❧

And other favorites

The Absinthe House

Crab Meat Ravigotte

6   tablespoons butter

3   green onions, chopped

1/2 small green pepper, chopped

1   5 ounce can mushrooms

1   pound lump crab meat

1   pimiento, finely chopped

1   tablespoon parsley, chopped

1/2 teaspoon white pepper

1/2 teaspoon celery seed

3   ounces dry sherry

1/2 cup bread crumbs

Sauté onions, green pepper and mushrooms lightly in butter until softened. Add crab meat, pimiento, seasonings and sherry. Toss gently, but do not break up crab meat lumps. Stir in half of the bread crumbs and put into individual oven proof baking dishes. Top with remaining bread crumbs and place under broiler until top begins to brown. Serve with toast points. Serves 4.

Fried Fantail Shrimp in Beer Batter

1   cup sifted flour

1/2 teaspoon sugar

1/2 teaspoon salt

     Dash of pepper

     Dash of nutmeg

1   teaspoon baking powder

1   egg, beaten

1   cup beer

2   pounds fresh shrimp

     Cooking oil

Stir all ingredients, except shrimp, into a batter. Peel shell from shrimp, leaving the last section and tail intact. Cut almost through shrimp at the center back without cutting ends. Dry shrimp and dip into beer batter. Fry in deep, hot fat until golden brown. Drain and serve at once. Serves 4.

Crawfish Étouffée

8 pounds fresh crawfish, washed
8 tablespoons butter
6 medium onions, chopped
1/2 cup celery, chopped
1/2 teaspoon tomato paste
1/2 cup water
1/2 teaspoon corn starch
   Salt, pepper and cayenne to taste
2 tablespoons green onions, chopped
2 tablespoons parsley, minced

Place crawfish in large container of boiling water. Remove from heat and let stand for 5 minutes. Drain, remove heads, peel and devein. In large saucepan, melt butter. Add onions, celery and tomato paste. Cook until tender. Add crawfish tails. In a small bowl, combine water and corn starch. Stir into onion mixture, stirring constantly. Add salt, pepper and cayenne. Bring to a boil and cook 10 minutes. Add onion tops and parsley. Serve over rice or pasta. Serves 4.

Deep Fried Soft Shelled Crabs

   Soft shelled crabs (1 or 2 per person)
1 cup milk
1/2 cup water
2 eggs, beaten
   Seasoned flour
   Salt and cayenne pepper to taste
   Cooking oil

To clean soft shelled crabs, lift up pointed end of shell and remove the spongy debris inside. With a sharp knife, cut out eyes and mouth of crab. Turn over and remove the apron from the underside of the crab. Wash in cold water. In a bowl, mix milk, water, eggs, salt and pepper to taste. Dip each crab into the milk, then dredge in seasoned flour. Deep fry until golden brown. Garnish with lemon.

Deep Fried Soft Shelled Crabs

Scampi Mediterranean

Scallops in Garlic Butter

1 pound scallops

1/2 cup butter, melted

1½ teaspoons each chives and parsley, chopped

1/4 teaspoon tarragon

1/4 teaspoon garlic salt

1/2 teaspoon onion salt

 Dash of black pepper

 Dry bread crumbs, finely ground

Mix butter and seasonings. If scallops are large, cut into pieces. If small, leave whole. Arrange 4 to 6 small baking dishes on a baking sheet. Place some of the butter mixture in bottom of each dish. Put equal portions of scallops into each dish, then top with remaining butter mixture. Sprinkle with crumbs. Bake at 350 degrees for 10 minutes. Serve hot as an appetizer or as a luncheon entree. Serves 4 to 6.

Scampi Mediterranean

12 large shrimp, cleaned and deveined

4 cloves garlic, minced

 Butter

1/2 lemon

1/4 cup white wine

1 pound cooked fresh spinach

Sauté shrimp and garlic in butter for 3 minutes. Add wine and lemon juice. Cook in preheated oven at 375 degrees for 10 minutes. Serve over a bed of cooked spinach. Serves 2.

In the day and night city of "Nar'lens", there is no such concept as "too late." Likewise, slowness in all things, such as rocking on the front porch, swatting flies on the balcony or cooking a mess of greens, is greatly desired.

Night life in New Orleans

Lobster Savannah

4 small or 2 large lobsters, cooked
1/2 cup butter
1/2 bell pepper, finely chopped
1/2 small onion, finely chopped
1/2 pound mushrooms, sliced
1/2 cup flour
2 cups milk, warmed
1 tablespoon pimiento
Salt and white pepper to taste
1/4 cup sherry
1/4 cup Parmesan cheese, grated
Sprinkle of paprika

Sauté pepper and onion in butter. Add mushrooms and continue to cook, about 5 more minutes. Stir in flour. Heat milk separately and add gradually, stirring to keep consistency smooth. Add pimiento, salt and pepper to taste. Bring to a simmer and add sherry. Cut lobsters in half and remove meat. Cut meat into neat pieces. Add meat to sauce and heat through. Stuff lobster shell with above ingredients. Top with grated Parmesan cheese and paprika and put into oven to brown. Serves 4.

Artichoke and Oyster Casserole

4 cups milk
1 cup half and half
1 cup butter, softened
1 cup flour
6 dozen oysters, drained
1 teaspoon black pepper
2 teaspoons salt
Dash hot pepper sauce
2 tablespoons Worcestershire sauce
1/2 cup sherry
8 fresh cooked artichoke hearts, finely chopped
Artichoke leaves
Bread crumbs

Mix milk and half and half together and warm over low heat. Melt butter and blend in flour. Remove from heat and slowly add milk and cream mixture, stirring to make roux (page 17). Heat oysters to remove excess liquid and add to the cream sauce. Simmer 5 minutes and stir in seasonings, sherry and artichoke hearts. Pour into a casserole dish, arrange artichoke leaves around the edge of dish, sprinkle with bread crumbs and bake for 10 minutes at 350 degrees. Serves 8.

Fried Catfish

Fried Catfish

1   pound catfish fillets
1/2   teaspoon salt
      Dash of freshly ground pepper
1/2   teaspoon paprika
2   eggs
1   tablespoon water
1   cup cornmeal
3   tablespoons butter

Sprinkle fillets with salt, pepper and paprika. Beat eggs and stir in water. Spread cornmeal on a piece of waxed paper. Roll each piece of fish in cornmeal. Next, dip it in the egg mixture and roll in cornmeal again. Refrigerate fish for about 20 minutes. Melt butter in a skillet over low heat and fry fish for about 3 minutes on each side, adding more butter if needed. Serves 4.

Crab Meat Quiche

      Pastry for a single crust 9" pie
1   tablespoon butter
1   tablespoon celery, chopped
1   tablespoon onions, chopped
1 1/2   cups crab meat, picked over well to remove shell or cartilage
2   tablespoons parsley, chopped
2   tablespoons sherry
4   eggs, lightly beaten
1   cup milk
1   cup cream
1/4   teaspoon nutmeg, grated
1/2   teaspoon salt
1/4   teaspoon white pepper

Preheat oven to 375 degrees. Line a 9" pie pan with pastry and line pastry with foil. Add dried beans to weight the bottom down and bake 30 minutes. Remove the foil and beans. Melt butter in a skillet and sauté the celery and onions until wilted. Add the crab meat and cook over high heat until any liquid has evaporated. Stir in the parsley and sherry. Sprinkle the inside of the baked pastry shell with the crab meat mixture.

Combine eggs, milk, cream, nutmeg, salt and pepper and pour over the crab mixture in the pie. Bake 40 minutes, or until knife inserted comes out clean. Cut into wedges and serve immediately. Serves 6.

Scalloped Oysters

2   pints (4 cups) medium oysters, drained and picked over
      Strained oyster liquid with milk *or* cream added to make 2 cups
3   cups crumbled crackers
1/2   cup melted butter
      Salt and pepper to taste

Butter a shallow casserole dish and arrange 2 layers of oysters in it, with cracker crumbs between layers and on top. Sprinkle each layer with salt and pepper. Pour melted butter over the casserole, then add oyster liquid, trickling the mixture around the edges of the casserole until it rises up around the top layer. Bake at 400 degrees for 20 minutes or until browned. Serves 8.

Trout Marguery

1   2 1/2 pound trout
1   tablespoon olive oil
1   cup water
2   egg yolks
      Juice of 1 lemon, strained
1/2   cup butter
      Dash of salt, pepper and cayenne
12   shrimp
2   truffles, cut into small pieces
1/2   can mushrooms, chopped

Skin and fillet trout and place the folded fillets in a pan with olive oil and water. Bake in oven at 350 degrees for 15 minutes. To make Hollandaise sauce, put beaten egg yolks and lemon juice in a double boiler over hot water and gradually add melted butter, stirring constantly until thickened. Add seasoning, shrimp, truffles and mushrooms to sauce and pour over fish. Serves 2.

Relaxing in the French Quarter

Shrimp Creole

3	tablespoons butter *or* bacon drippings
2	cups onions, coarsely chopped
2	cloves garlic, finely minced
3	ribs celery, coarsely chopped
1	green pepper, cored, seeded and chopped
3	ripe tomatoes, cored and peeled
1	bay leaf
2	sprigs fresh thyme *or* 1/2 teaspoon dried thyme
	Salt to taste
1/2	teaspoon ground black pepper
1/4	teaspoon cayenne pepper
2	pounds shrimp, peeled and deveined
1	teaspoon Worcestershire sauce (optional)
	Hot fluffy rice

Melt butter or bacon drippings in a large saucepan and sauté the onions, garlic, celery and green pepper until tender, but not browned. Add the tomatoes, bay leaf, thyme, salt, pepper and cayenne. Simmer 10 minutes, stirring occasionally. Add the shrimp and cover. Simmer 10 minutes. Season with Worcestershire, if desired. Serve with hot, fluffy rice. Serves 6.

Creole Seafood Seasoning

1/2	teaspoon ground black pepper
1/4	teaspoon cayenne pepper
1/2	teaspoon tarragon
1	teaspoon onion salt
1/2	teaspoon garlic powder
1	tablespoon paprika
1	teaspoon salt

Mix ingredients thoroughly. Use to flavor fish and shell fish, gumbos, soups, sauces and dressings.

White Remoulade Sauce

2   cups mayonnaise
1   tablespoon dark mustard
1/4   cup creamed horseradish
1/4   cup green onions, chopped
1/4   cup capers, chopped
1/4   cup gherkins (baby dill pickles), chopped
2   tablespoons parsley, chopped
2   tablespoons chervil, chopped
    Lemon juice to taste
    Salt and pepper to taste

Whisk together all ingredients and chill. For variety, white wine vinegar may be substituted for lemon; tarragon may be substituted for chervil or finely chopped hard boiled eggs may be added. Serve over fish, shell fish or green vegetables. Yields 3 cups.

Trout Amandine

2   fillets of trout
1/2   cup butter
4   tablespoons sliced almonds
    Juice of 1/2 lemon
1   teaspoon parsley, chopped

Sauté trout in 1/4 cup butter until golden brown and cooked through. Put aside and keep hot. Brown almonds in remaining 1/4 cup butter and add lemon juice. Pour over trout. Sprinkle with parsley and serve at once. Serves 2.

Crab Meat Imperial

1   green pepper, finely diced
2   pimientos, finely diced
1   tablespoon Dijon mustard
1   teaspoon salt
1/2   teaspoon white pepper
2   whole eggs
1   cup mayonnaise
3   pounds lump crab meat

Mix pepper and pimientos. Add mustard, salt, white pepper, eggs and mayonnaise. Mix well. Add crab meat, mixing gently so that lumps are not broken. Divide mixture into 6 crab shells or casseroles, heaping it in lightly. Top with a coating of mayonnaise and sprinkle with paprika. Bake at 350 degrees for 15 minutes. Serve hot or cold. Serves 6.

Shrimp Remoulade

3/4   cup olive oil
1/4   cup prepared mustard
1/4   cup wine vinegar
1   teaspoon salt
1/2   teaspoon paprika
1   hard-cooked egg, chopped
1/2   cup celery, minced
1   tablespoon onion, grated
2   tablespoons parsley, minced
1/2   tablespoon green pepper, minced
2   pounds shrimp, cooked, shelled and deveined

Whisk the oil, mustard, vinegar, salt and paprika thoroughly. Fold in the egg, celery, onion, parsley and green pepper. Add shrimp and chill for several hours until ready to serve. Serves 6.

Trout Amandine

Sea Bass Siciliana

Sea Bass Siciliana

2   6-8 ounce sea bass fillets

6   Roma tomatoes

2   garlic cloves, chopped

6   black Greek olives

1   tablespoon capers
     Olive oil

1/2 cup fish stock or clam juice

Sauté sea bass with chopped tomatoes and garlic in olive oil over medium heat for 5 minutes. Add fish stock or clam juice, olives and capers. Put into preheated 375 degree oven for 12 to 15 minutes or until fish is cooked through. Serves 2.

Creole Trinity Sauce

1   tablespoon vegetable oil

2   green onions, chopped

1   green bell pepper, cored, seeded
     and chopped

1   stalk celery, chopped

1   clove garlic, finely chopped

1   16 ounce can whole stewed tomatoes

1/2 teaspoon thyme, crumbled
     Pinch of ground hot red pepper

Heat oil in medium size saucepan over medium heat. Add green onions, pepper and celery. Sauté 5 minutes or until softened. Add garlic. Sauté 1 minute. Add tomatoes with their liquid, thyme and red pepper. Cover and simmer 10 minutes. Serve hot over vegetables, hamburgers or fish. Yields 2 cups.

Baked Seafood Salad

1/2	cup green pepper, chopped
1/4	cup onion, minced
1	cup celery, chopped
1	cup crab meat, cooked or canned
1	cup shrimp, cooked or canned
1	cup mayonnaise
1/2	teaspoon salt
1	teaspoon Worcestershire sauce
2	cups corn flakes, crushed, *or* 1 cup fine dry bread crumbs
	Dash of paprika
2	tablespoons butter or margarine
	lemon slices

Combine green pepper, onion, celery, fish, mayonnaise, salt and Worcestershire. Mix lightly. Place mixture into individual shells or shallow baking dish. Sprinkle with crushed corn flakes or crumbs and paprika. Dot with butter. Bake at 350 degrees about 30 minutes. Serve with slices of lemon. Serves 6.

Baked Fish Fillet
(Bass, flounder, snapper, swordfish, tuna or other)

2	pounds fish fillets
1/2	cup butter
	Lemon juice
1	tablespoon dry white wine
	Salt, pepper and paprika
1/4	cup Parmesan cheese

Place butter in shallow baking dish in hot oven (450 degrees) until it is browned. Salt and pepper fillets. Place fillets flesh side down in sizzling hot butter and return to oven for about 10 minutes. Turn with spatula and baste with pan juice. Sprinkle each piece with lemon juice and white wine, cheese and paprika. Return to oven until done, approximately 5 minutes. Run under broiler to brown cheese. Baste fish with sauce and serve in the sauce. Serves 4.

Deviled Crab

2	6 ounce packages frozen crab meat, thawed
2	tablespoons butter or margarine
1	cup medium white sauce (page 17)
1	teaspoon dry mustard
	Dash cayenne pepper or hot pepper sauce
1	tablespoon parsley, minced
1	teaspoon onion, minced
1	teaspoon Worcestershire sauce
1/2	cup sharp Cheddar cheese, grated

Sauté crab meat several minutes in butter. Add white sauce and seasonings, with more salt, if necessary. Fill individual shells or casseroles with the mixture and top with cheese. Bake until lightly browned on top, about 20 minutes, at 375 degrees. Serves 4.

Fillet of Sole with Pine Nuts

2	6 ounce fillets of sole
1½	tablespoons pine nuts
2	tablespoons unsalted butter
1½	teaspoons fresh chives, minced, *or* scallion greens
	Seafood seasoning
	Flour for dredging

Sauté pine nuts in 1 tablespoon butter over moderately high heat, stirring, until golden. Add chives or scallion greens. Remove from heat and transfer to a dish. Season flour with dried seafood seasoning (page 28). Season sole with salt and pepper and dredge in flour to coat. Heat remaining butter over moderately high heat and sauté sole 2 minutes per side, or until it flakes. Serve sole with pine nut sauce. Serves 2.

Louisiana's coastal gulf water used to have such massive quantities of oyster beds that ships had to avoid whole banks of them. People who lived near the water could spear more fish than they could eat, and shovel shell fish by the bushels.

Fettuccine San Remo

1	pound fettuccine pasta
3/4	pound medium shrimp, peeled and deveined
1/2	pound medium scallops
2	ounces fresh basil
3	cloves garlic, chopped
1/4	cup Olive oil
2	cups fish stock or clam juice
	Parsley
	Pine nuts

Sauté garlic in 1/4 cup olive oil for 1 minute. Add shrimp and scallops and cook for 4 minutes. Add basil, parsley and 2 cups fish stock or clam juice. Simmer for 10 minutes. Serve over cooked fettuccine. Top with pine nuts. Serves 4.

Shrimp and Mushroom Casserole

1 1/2	tablespoons butter or margarine
2	teaspoons onion, chopped
2	teaspoons green pepper, chopped
2	tablespoons flour
3/4	cup half and half (cream and milk)
1/4	teaspoon paprika
1/2	teaspoon salt
1/2	cup shredded cheese
1	6 ounce can mushrooms, quartered
1	pound shrimp, boiled and cleaned
	Buttered bread crumbs

Melt butter or margarine; add onion and green pepper. Cook until tender but not brown. Add flour and blend. Add remaining ingredients, except bread crumbs and pour into a buttered casserole dish. Top with bread crumbs and bake at 350 degrees for 20 minutes. Serves 4.

Shrimp Mold

Molded Shrimp Salad

1-2 **pounds fresh shrimp, unpeeled,** *or* **24 ounces (3 cups) peeled shrimp**
1 **envelope unflavored gelatin**
   Juice of 1 lemon
2 **tablespoons cold water**
1 **cup sour cream**
1 **8 ounce package cream cheese, softened**
1/2 **cup mayonnaise**
1/2 **medium bell pepper, diced**
1 **stalk celery, finely chopped**
2 **green onions, finely chopped**
1 **2 ounce jar pimientos, chopped and drained**
   Salt and white pepper to taste
2 **teaspoons Worcestershire sauce**
   Watercress, lettuce and olives for garnish

Peel shrimp. Bring a large pot of salted water to a boil. Add shrimp; cook until pink, about 2 minutes. Do not overcook. Drain and rinse in cold water. Soften gelatin in lemon juice and cold water. Melt over low heat and reserve. Chop shrimp in small bits. Add sour cream, cream cheese and mayonnaise and whisk until smooth. Stir in remaining ingredients, except gelatin. Add gelatin and stir until well blended. Oil a 5-1/2 cup ring mold or fish mold. Pour shrimp mixture into mold. Cover with plastic wrap and refrigerate 8 hours or overnight. Carefully warm outside of mold and turn out onto serving platter. Garnish with watercress, lettuce or olives and serve with crackers. Yields appetizer serving for 12 or luncheon entree for 6.

Shrimp Casserole

1 **pound shrimp, shelled and deveined**
2 **tablespoons butter**
1/2 **teaspoon dry mustard**
4 **slices bread, crusts removed**
1½ **cups Gruyere cheese, grated**
2 **eggs, beaten**
1 **cup milk**
1/2 **teaspoon salt**
   Ground pepper to taste

Preheat oven to 350 degrees. Cook shrimp, covered, in 1/2 cup water 5 minutes. Drain, reserving the broth. Cream the butter with the mustard and spread on the bread. Cut into cubes. Arrange the bread cubes, cheese and shrimp in layers in a greased 1 quart casserole. Mix the eggs, milk, reserved shrimp broth, salt and pepper and pour over the shrimp mixture. Set in a pan of hot water and bake 1 hour or until a knife inserted in the center comes out clean. Serve immediately. Serves 4.

Baked Stuffed Flounder

4	flounders, medium size
1/2	celery, chopped
1/2	cup green onions, chopped
1	clove garlic, minced
8	tablespoons butter
1	cup bread crumbs
4	tablespoons lemon juice
1/2	pound boiled shrimp, chopped
1/2	pound lump crab meat
2	tablespoons parsley, chopped
1	egg, slightly beaten
	Salt, black pepper and cayenne to taste

Sauté celery, onion and garlic in melted butter over low heat. Add bread, crab, shrimp, parsley and egg. Mix well. Season with salt and pepper. Split the thick side of the founder lengthwise and crosswise. Loosen meat from bone of fish to form a pocket for stuffing. Brush well with melted butter and lemon juice. Sprinkle salt and pepper over fish and stuff pocket. Place in pan with enough water to cover bottom of pan. Broil 3" from heat until fish flakes easily with a fork. Baste frequently with liquid in pan. Serves 4.

"It is unseasonable and unwholesome in all months that have not an R in their names to eat an oyster."

... William Butler

Crab Cakes

1	pound crab meat, picked over
1/4	cup onion diced
1/4	cup red bell pepper, diced
3	cups fresh bread crumbs
1/2	cup mayonnaise
1/4	cup cream cheese, softened
1	tablespoon Dijon mustard
1	egg, slightly beaten
1/2	teaspoon dried leaf tarragon
1/8	teaspoon cayenne pepper
1/8	teaspoon salt
2	tablespoons vegetable oil
	Lemon wedges or slices to serve

Drain crab meat well. Combine crab meat, onion, bell pepper and 1/2 cup of the bread crumbs in a medium size bowl. Beat mayonnaise, cream cheese, mustard, egg, tarragon, cayenne and salt together in a separate bowl. Stir mayonnaise mixture into crab meat mixture. Cover and refrigerate 30 minutes. Place remaining crumbs into a shallow bowl. Using an oval soup spoon, drop spoonfuls of mixture onto crumbs and form into patties, coating each side with crumbs. Heat oil in a skillet over medium heat. Carefully add crab cakes. Cook until golden brown, turning once. If oil browns, wipe out skillet and add fresh oil. Serve with lemon. Makes 24 appetizer size crab cakes or 6 entree size cakes.

Crab Cakes

Po' Boy Sandwich

Frogs' Legs Provençale

24 jumbo frogs' legs, trimmed
    milk
    flour seasoned with salt and pepper
    Olive oil
3   tablespoons butter
1   garlic clove, finely chopped
    Lemon juice to taste
    finely chopped parsley

Soak the frogs' legs in water to cover for 2 hours. Drain and dry well. Dip the frogs' legs in milk, then dredge in seasoned flour. Add oil to a skillet to the depth of 1/4 inch. When it's hot, cook the frogs' legs on all sides, 6 to 8 minutes. Transfer the frogs' legs to a hot plate and pour off and discard the oil from the skillet. Add the butter to the skillet and cook to golden brown. Add the garlic, then pour the butter over the frogs' legs. Sprinkle with lemon juice and chopped parsley and serve immediately. Serves 6.

36

Po' Boy Sandwich

2   dozen oysters, deep fried *or* shrimp *or* other
    seafood
    Remoulade sauce (page 29) *or* mayonnaise *or*
    tartar sauce
1/2 head lettuce, shredded
1   crusty French loaf, unsliced
    lemon slices optional

Slice loaf horizontally. Spread bottom half with Remoulade sauce or mayonnaise. Pile on the deep fried oysters. Top with lettuce and thinly sliced lemon, if desired. Cover with top half of loaf. Cut in half crosswise, or quarters for serving 2 or more.

Legend holds that the Po' Boy, a succulent, mouth-watering working man's food, was also sold on the streets late at night for revelers who had over indulged with drink and jazz.

Meats

Veal Chop
Marsala

Southern
Fried
Chicken

Rack of
Lamb

Baked
Chicken
with
Vegetables

And other
favorites

On the River Front

Pork Loin Roast with Yam-Stuffed Apples

1	pork loin roast, about 6 pounds
	Salt, pepper and sage
6-8	large tart baking apples
1	16 ounce can sweet potatoes
1/4	cup brown sugar
1	teaspoon salt
1/4	teaspoon cinnamon
1/2	cup almonds, slivered
1/4	cup butter, melted
1/4	cup maple syrup

Rub pork with 1/2 teaspoon salt per pound. Sprinkle with pepper and sage. Place roast, fat side up, on rack in an open pan. Do not add water. Roast uncovered at 300 degrees for 4 to 4-1/2 hours or until well done. Wash and core apples. Remove enough pulp to make core opening about 1-1/4" wide. Mash sweet potatoes. Combine with apple pulp, brown sugar, salt, cinnamon and one half of the almonds. Blend butter and syrup in saucepan and spoon a little of the syrup mixture into the apple cavities. Fill cavities with sweet potato mixture. Mound a spoonful on top of each apple. Stud stuffing with remaining almonds. Place apples around roast or in separate dish the last 1-1/2 hours of baking time. Baste apples occasionally with remaining syrup. When roast is done, arrange apples and roast on heated serving platter. Serves 6.

Hollandaise Sauce

4 egg yolks
2 tablespoons lemon juice
1/2 pound (1 cup) butter, melted
1/4 teaspoon salt
   Dash cayenne pepper

In top half of double boiler, beat egg yolks and stir in lemon juice. Cook very slowly in double boiler over low heat, never allowing water in bottom pan to come to a boil. Add butter, a dribble at a time. Stir constantly with a wooden spoon. Add salt and pepper. Continue cooking slowly until thickened, about 5 minutes. Sauce will thicken more as it cools. If heat is too high or sauce stands too long over heat, it may curdle. It can be made smooth again by very slowly adding 1 tablespoon boiling water and whisking until sauce reconstitutes. Yields 1 cup.

Veal Oscar

6 5 ounce veal cutlets from top round
8 fresh mushrooms, sliced
4 tablespoons butter
1½ cups Hollandaise sauce
1 pound lump crab meat
2 green jumbo asparagus

Cook asparagus in salt water. Let cool. Sauté mushrooms in 4 tablespoons butter. Add crab meat and toss gently 3 or 4 minutes. Dust veal cutlets in flour. Brown quickly on each side, and finish cooking at medium-low about 10 minutes each side. Place on 6 plates with 2 asparagus spears; 1 on each side of veal. Cover veal with crab meat. Top with Hollandaise sauce and glaze under broiler. Serve at once. Serves 6.

Stuffed Pork Chops

8 pork chops
3 cups bread crumbs
1/4 cup celery, diced
1 cup oysters, chopped
   Salt and pepper

1/2 cup oyster liquid
1/4 cup onions, diced
1 cup crab meat
2 eggs

Sauté celery lightly. Combine all dry ingredients with crab meat, oysters, oyster liquid and eggs. Mix well. Place about 1 cup of stuffing between two pork chops and bake on a greased baking pan. Bake for 20 minutes at 350 degrees. Serve with a brown sauce. (Page 17). Serves 4.

Hoppin' John

3 cups dried blackeyed peas
1/2 pound salt pork, with rind removed
1 onion, chopped
1 bay leaf
   Salt to taste
   Pinch of crushed red pepper
1 cup rice, uncooked

Soak the peas overnight in water to cover. Drain. Cook the salt pork in 4 cups boiling water for 30 minutes. Add the peas, onion, bay leaf, salt and red pepper. Simmer for 1 hour. Add the rice and simmer slowly 20 to 30 minutes, or until rice is done and peas are soft. Add more water if needed. (Chicken broth may be used instead of water). Adjust seasonings to taste. Serves 6.

Hoppin' John

Southern Fried Chicken

Southern Fried Chicken with Cream Gravy

1   3 pound frying chicken cut into serving pieces
1   cup milk or buttermilk
1   cup flour
1   teaspoon salt
1/2 teaspoon white pepper
    Shortening for frying

Wash chicken pieces and soak in milk or buttermilk for 30 minutes. Drain but do not dry. Sprinkle salt liberally on both sides. Place the flour, pepper and 1 teaspoon salt into a medium size brown paper bag. Add chicken; close top of bag and shake so all pieces are coated evenly and well. Remove chicken pieces and shake to remove excess flour. Put on rack and dry about 20 minutes. Heat shortening in a large skillet. Hold on high heat for a few minutes until fat is crackling hot. Carefully place chicken pieces in skillet side by side, fleshy side down. Cook rapidly a few minutes, making sure pieces have a firm but very light brown crust on the bottom. Turn each piece as it reaches this stage until all are turned. Continue cooking one minute over high heat. Reduce heat to low and cover skillet. Cook 20 to 30 minutes until heated through. Remove cover and turn heat up again to highest level. Turn each piece as

the bottom becomes golden, but not too brown, and quite crisp. The top surface of the chicken pieces will have a soft, dispirited look when the cover is removed, but a couple of minutes of high heat crisping will restore the pieces to golden crispness. Remove pieces to drain on paper towels. Serve with chicken cream gravy and hot biscuits (page 59). Serves 4 to 6.

Chicken Cream Gravy

3   tablespoons cooking fat from chicken
3   tablespoons flour
    Freshly ground black pepper
2   dashes hot pepper sauce
2   cups milk

Drain fat left in the skillet after frying chicken through a sieve. Return 3 tablespoons fat to skillet, along with the brown particles remaining in the sieve. Turn the heat to high, add the flour and stir, picking up browned bits remaining in skillet. When flour is medium brown, turn heat off. Add a generous sprinkle of the pepper and the hot sauce. Pour in the milk all at once. Turn heat to medium high and stir constantly until gravy thickens. The consistency should be similar to heavy cream. Yields 2 cups.

Veal Chop Marsala

Red Ham Loaf

1 1/2   pounds ground ham
1   pound ground pork shoulder
1/8   teaspoon black pepper
2   eggs
1/2   cup canned tomatoes
2/3   cup milk
2/3   cup cracker crumbs
        Salt to taste
1   cup brown sugar
2   teaspoons powdered mustard
1/3   cup vinegar
1/2   cup water

Mix ham, pork, pepper, eggs, tomatoes, milk, cracker crumbs and salt. Shape into a loaf and place in loaf baking pan. Make basting sauce by combining brown sugar, mustard, vinegar and water. Bring to a boil and boil for 2 minutes. Baste with this sauce every 15 minutes until done. Bake at 350 degrees for 1 hour. Serves 6 to 8.

Veal Chop Marsala

2   veal chops
8   large mushrooms, sliced
2   tablespoons butter
1/2   cup Marsala wine
2   tablespoons parsley, chopped
        Salt and pepper
        Flour for thickening

Sauté mushrooms in butter over medium heat. Add 1/4 cup Marsala wine. Cook for 3 minutes. Add parsley, salt and pepper. Thicken with 1 tablespoon flour mixed with 1 or 2 tablespoons additional wine (or water) , if needed. Grill or broil veal chops approximately 10 minutes on one side then turn and grill until done on other side. Test doneness by making a tiny slit in the meat. Pour sauce over grilled veal chops. Serves 2.

Old English Prime Rib
or Standing Rib Roast

1/2   pound per serving
2   tablespoons Worcestershire sauce
1   teaspoon paprika
    Salt and pepper
    Rock salt (ice cream salt)

Select "Choice" prime rib or standing rib. Season with Worcestershire sauce, paprika and salt and pepper. Rub seasoning into the meat. In a large, heavy pan, pour a layer of rock salt until the bottom surface of the container is completely covered. Lightly dampen the rock salt with water until the salt is just moist. Place the prime rib onto the salt in a standing rib position. Cover the remaining portion of the meat completely with the rock salt and again dampen all salt lightly with water. Do not cover the roast pan. Place roast, covered only with salt, into oven, preheated to 500 degrees. Allow meat to roast for 15 minutes per pound. When cooking time is completed, remove roast from the oven. The salt will be very hard and must be carefully broken away from the meat. Using a wooden mallet, gently strike the surface of the salt, creating cracks. Pull the salt sections away from the meat. This process does not impart a salt taste but traps vital flavor juices and insures minimum shrinkage of the meat.

Baby Lamb Rack Amandine

4   baby racks of lamb 1 pound each
    Salt and pepper
1/2   cup dry vermouth
1   cup blanched sliced almonds, toasted

Roast lamb at 350 degrees to desired doneness, about 30 to 40 minutes. Remove the excess fat from the pan. Add dry vermouth to dissolve brown specks left in the pan. Let sauce cook until it is reduced by half. Cover the lamb racks with toasted almonds. Pour sauce over racks, slice into chops and serve. Serves 4.

Virginia Roast Country Ham

Virginia Roast Country Ham

Country ham is cured with salt, not sugar. It is smoked, chewy and salty. Country ham is often served with red eye gravy which is made with the ham drippings and coffee.

1   10 to 12 pound country ham

Soak the ham overnight in cold water to cover. Preheat oven to 500 degrees. Scrub ham to remove the pepper coating and any mold that may by present. Place ham in a covered roaster with 6 cups cold water. Bake ham 20 minutes. Turn oven off. Allow ham to remain in oven without opening door for 3 hours. Turn oven heat to 500 degrees and leave on for 15 minutes. Turn off the heat and allow ham to remain in oven for at least 3 hours or more, or overnight. Remove ham from roaster and cut off the rind. Ham is ready to serve or may be glazed, if desired.

Red Eye Gravy

> **Roast pan drippings**
>
> 1/2   cup coffee
>
> 1/2   water
>
> 1/4   cup cream (optional)

Put roast pan on low heat and slowly add coffee and water. Stir well, scraping drippings into gravy. The gravy will be dark red and salty. For richer gravy, add cream with coffee and water. Serve with ham, grits, eggs and biscuits.

If you carry an Irish potato in your pocket, it will cure rheumatism. To cure a wart, take a green pea, cut it, and rub it on the wart. Then take the pea and wrap it in a piece of paper and throw it away. The person who picks it up will get the wart.

-Louisiana Folklore

Roast Chicken with Vegetables

Stuffed Flank Steak

1   flank steak, 1-1/2 pounds, well scored
2½ cups coarse bread crumbs
1/2 cup celery, chopped
2   tablespoons onions, chopped
1   tablespoon green pepper, chopped
1   teaspoon salt
1/4 cup butter, melted
1   egg
     Salt pork or bacon strips

Blend bread crumbs, celery, onion and pepper. Add salt and melted butter and enough hot water to moisten slightly. Add egg. Spread dressing on flank steak and roll up lengthwise. Tie. Brown on all sides in hot fat. Place in heavy kettle or casserole and lay strips of salt pork or bacon over the top. Cover and cook in oven at 325 degrees for 1-1/2 to 2 hours. Slice and serve with mushroom gravy. Serves 4.

Honey Glazed Chicken

1/2 cup honey
2   tablespoons vegetable oil
2   tablespoons prepared mustard
2   tablespoons lemon juice
1/2 teaspoon grated lemon peel
1/2 teaspoon salt
2½ pound broiler-fryer chicken, cut up

Mix all ingredients except chicken. Cover and grill chicken, bone sides down, 6" from medium coals, about 30 minutes, turning frequently. Brush chicken several times with honey mixture and continue cooking until chicken is done, 20 to 40 minutes more. Serves 6.

44

Chicken Country Captain

1   bunch parsley, chopped
4   green peppers, chopped
2   large onions, chopped
1   clove garlic, minced
    Cooking oil
2   fryers, cut in pieces
    Seasoned flour (salt, pepper, paprika)
2   16 ounce cans tomatoes
1   teaspoon mace
2   teaspoons curry powder
    Salt and pepper to taste
1/2 box currants
    Cooked rice
1/2 pound blanched almonds

Fry parsley, green peppers and onions in cooking oil slowly for 15 minutes. Add garlic. Stir in tomatoes, mace, curry, salt and pepper. Dredge chicken in seasoned flour. In a separate skillet, fry until brown. Place chicken and sauce in a baking dish and cook slowly in oven at 275 degrees for 1-1/2 to 2 hours. Add currants 1/2 hour before serving. Arrange rice on a large platter, pour sauce over rice and place pieces of chicken on top. Sprinkle toasted almonds over chicken. Serves 8.

Classic Roast Chicken With Vegetables

1   4-5 pound roasting or frying chicken
    A bouquet of fresh herbs for stuffing (sprigs of rosemary, thyme, basil or sage)
2   cups chicken stock or broth
2   varieties of summer squash, diced large
2   bell peppers, quartered
10 small red potatoes, halved
4   large carrots, halved
1   large sweet onion, quartered
3   tablespoons flour
1/2 cup milk or cream
    Salt and freshly ground black pepper

Preheat oven to 400 degrees. Rinse the chicken and pat dry. Place bunch of herbs into body of chicken. Tie or skewer legs together. Tuck wing tips under breast. Place the chicken in a roasting pan large enough to hold the chicken and the vegetables which will be added later. Pour the broth around the chicken and roast for 20 minutes per pound, basting occasionally. During last 45 minutes of cooking, arrange vegetables around chicken, baste and return to oven. When chicken and vegetables are done, remove to a large serving platter and cover with foil to keep warm. Skim excess fat from pan drippings. Stir flour and milk in a small bowl and add to the remaining cooking liquid. Heat over stove to a boil then reduce heat and continue to stir until gravy is thickened. Season with salt and pepper. Serve hot in a gravy dish along with chicken and vegetables. Serves 6.

Savory Meat Loaf

1   pound ground beef
1/2 pound ground veal
1/2 pound ground pork
3/4 cup cracker crumbs
1/2 cup celery, diced
1/4 cup parsley, minced
3/4 teaspoon salt
1/4 teaspoon pepper
3/4 cup milk
1   egg, slightly beaten
1/4 cup catsup
3   green pepper rings
    Parsley sprigs (optional)

Combine first 3 ingredients; stir well. Add cracker crumbs and next 7 ingredients; stir well. Shape into a 9" x 6" loaf and place on a lightly oiled rack of a broiler pan. Spread tops and sides with catsup. Bake at 350 degrees for 1 hour and 20 minutes. Top with green pepper rings. Bake additional 10 minutes. Garnish with parsley, if desired. Serves 8.

Barbecued Ribs

4   1/2 pound racks of fresh pork loin back ribs
3   cups water
1/2   cup soy sauce
2   tablespoons cornstarch

Place pork back ribs in Dutch oven; add water. Heat to boiling; reduce heat. Cover and simmer 5 minutes. Remove ribs; drain. Return to Dutch oven. Mix soy sauce and corn starch; brush on ribs. Continue brushing both sides of ribs with soy sauce mixture every 10 minutes, until mixture is gone, about 30 minutes. Grill ribs about 6" from medium coals, brushing with barbecue sauce (recipe follows) every 3 minutes, until ribs are done and meat begins to pull away from the bone, about 20 minutes. Cut into serving pieces. Serve with remaining sauce. Serves 4.

Barbecue Sauce

1   cup water
1   cup catsup
1/4   cup packed brown sugar
1/4   cup vinegar
1/4   cup Worcestershire sauce
1   tablespoon celery seed
1   teaspoon chili powder
1   teaspoon salt
      Few drops of red pepper sauce
      Dash of pepper

Heat all ingredients to boiling. Simmer 10 minutes. This sauce may be used on pork, chicken or beef.

Pork Chops and Rice Casserole

4   pork chops
2   tablespoons shortening
1   cup uncooked rice
1   16 ounce can tomatoes
1   onion, sliced
1   can beef consomme
1   teaspoon thyme
      Salt and pepper

Brown pork chops in a small amount of shortening. In a greased 1-1/2 quart casserole, place uncooked rice and lay cooked pork chops over rice. Add the other ingredients and cook at 350 degrees for 1 hour. Serves 4

Baked Pork Chops with Apple Stuffing

6   double loin pork chops

3   medium apples, finely chopped

1/2   cup brown sugar

1   teaspoon ground cinnamon

1/2   teaspoon ground nutmeg

3   cups hot water

1   carrot, finely chopped

1   medium onion, finely chopped

2   stalks celery, finely chopped

1   teaspoon salt

    Few grains pepper

Cut deep pockets in chops. Combine apples, brown sugar, cinnamon and nutmeg. Fill pockets with apple mixture Place chops, stuffing side up, in baking pan. Pour water around chops. Add carrot, onion, celery, salt and pepper to water. Bake in moderate oven at 350 degrees for 1-1/2 hours. Thicken gravy if desired. Serves 6.

Old-Fashioned Pot Roast and Potatoes

1   3 pound boneless beef chuck roast

6   tablespoons flour, divided

6   tablespoons butter or margarine, divided

3   cups hot water

2   teaspoons beef bouillon base

1   medium onion, quartered

1   celery rib, cut into 1" pieces

1   teaspoon salt

1/2   teaspoon pepper

4   carrots, cut into 2" pieces

4   medium potatoes, quartered

Sprinkle the roast with 1 tablespoon flour. In a Dutch oven, brown the roast on all sides in half of the butter. Add water, beef base, onion, celery, salt and pepper. Bring to a boil. Reduce heat. Cover and simmer 1 hour. Add carrots and potatoes. Cover and simmer 1 hour longer or until meat is tender. Remove meat, carrots and potatoes to a serving platter and keep warm. Strain cooking juices; set aside. Melt remaining butter. Stir in remaining flour. Cook until thickened and gradually add 2 cups of the cooking liquid and blend until smooth. Cook and stir until gravy reaches desired consistency. Serves 6.

Filet de Boeuf with Bearnaise Sauce

1   whole beef tenderloin roast, 4 to 5 pounds

2   tablespoons butter

1   16 ounce can beef broth

Rub beef with butter. Baste with broth. Bake at 350 degrees for 20 to 25 minutes (for rare) or 35 minutes (for medium). Serve on a platter with canned or cooked new potatoes browned in butter, warmed cherry tomatoes and fresh green beans. To serve, pool individual serving plates with a scoop of Bearnaise Sauce and slices of tenderloin. Surround with vegetables.

Bearnaise Sauce

3/4   cup vermouth

1   tablespoon vinegar

1   green onion, chopped

1   tablespoon parsley, finely chopped

1   teaspoon tarragon, finely chopped

    Pinch of chervil

2   peppercorns

1   cup butter

3   egg yolks

Combine vermouth, vinegar, onion, parsley, tarragon, chervil and peppercorns. Cook until the mixture is reduced to one half volume. Cool. Melt butter and beat egg yolks. Add butter and egg yolks alternately to first mixture, stirring constantly. Remove mixture from heat. Beat with a wooden spoon or wire whisk, then return to heat to thicken. Continue beating until sauce is the consistency of whipping cream. Yields about 1 cup.

Roast Crown of Lamb

Roast Crown of Lamb

2   loin roasts, containing 14 chops, cut and tied
    together to form crown
2   cups packaged poultry stuffing (optional)

Roast in a shallow pan at 325 degrees about 30 minutes per pound, approximately 2 hours. To prevent tips of bones from blackening, cover with a cube of salt pork or bread, or wrap with a piece of aluminum foil. For stuffed roast, allow 1/2 hour more cooking. Let roast set 15 minutes before carving. Carve into individual chops, allowing 2 or 3 ribs per person. Serve with oven roasted potatoes or parsley potatoes and mixed vegetables. Serves 4 to 6.

Chicken Fricassee

1   4 pound chicken, cut up
    Salt, pepper and flour
1   tablespoon shortening
1   onion, chopped
1   sprig thyme
1   tablespoon parsley, minced
1   bay leaf
3   cups boiling water

Season chicken with salt and pepper and coat with flour. Brown in shortening, add onion and sauté. Add seasonings and water. Bring to a boil, cover and reduce heat. Simmer until tender, about 1 hour. Serves 6.

Muffuletta Sandwich Feast

1   jar (16 ounces) marinated mixed vegetables, drained and coarsely chopped
1/4   cup green olives with pimiento, finely chopped
1   tablespoon olive oil
1   clove garlic, finely chopped
1/4   teaspoon leaf oregano, crumbled
1   10" round loaf crusty bread, unsliced
4   ounces Italian ham, thinly sliced
4   ounces Genoa salami, thinly sliced
4   ounces Provolone cheese, thinly sliced

Combine mixed vegetables and olives in small bowl. Heat oil in small saucepan over medium-low heat. Add garlic and oregano. Cook 2 minutes. Do not brown. Halve bread horizontally. Pull out some of bread from each half. Brush inside of bottom half with oil mixture. Top with half of vegetables. Add ham, salami and cheese slices. Top with other half of vegetables. Cover with top half of bread. Wrap sandwich in plastic wrap. Refrigerate 2 hours or overnight. Cut into 4 wedges to serve. Serves 2-4.

Entertainment in the French Quarter

Stuffed Peppers

Stuffed Peppers

6   large red or green peppers
1   pound ground beef
1   small onion, chopped
4   medium tomatoes, chopped, or 1 can
    tomatoes
1   cup cooked rice
    Seasonings as desired
1   cup tomato juice

Remove top and seeds from peppers. Parboil peppers 5 minutes. Brown meat and drain; add remaining ingredients. Mix well. Stuff peppers. Place in baking dish, pour tomato juice around peppers and bake at 350 degrees for 1 hour. Serves 6.

Ginger-Lime Marinade
For chicken, shrimp, fish or pork

1/2 cup lime juice
2   tablespoons vegetable oil
1   teaspoon fresh ginger root, finely chopped
1/4 teaspoon salt
1   garlic clove, minced
     Dash of ground red pepper (cayenne)

Mix all ingredients in shallow dish. Place seafood, poultry or pork in dish. Turn to coat all sides with marinade. Cover and refrigerate for 1 hour or longer. Yields 3/4 cup.

Quails With Wild Rice

10   quails
1   stick butter (1/2 cup)
1½   pounds chicken livers
2   large onions, chopped
1   green pepper, chopped
2   garlic cloves, minced
1½   sticks butter (3/4 cups)
2½   cups cooked wild rice
2   cups chicken broth
1½   cups port wine

Tie or skewer body cavity of quail. Sauté in 1 stick of butter until browned. Place in baking dish. Cover dish and bake at 325 degrees about 30 minutes. Sauté livers, onions, pepper and garlic in 1-1/2 sticks butter. Do not let vegetables brown, but cook to a clear color. Add cooked rice, chicken broth and wine. Place mixture in 3-quart baking dish. Cover and bake at 325 degrees about twenty minutes or until liquid is absorbed. Serve quail over rice. Variation: Quail may be lightly browned and placed on top of stuffing in baking pan. Mix chicken broth and wine and pour over quail and stuffing. Cover and bake at 350 degrees about 30 minutes. Serves 5 to 6.

Desserts & Sweets

Bananas Foster

❧

Bread Pudding with Whisky Sauce

❧

Pecan Pralines

❧

White Coconut Cake

❧

And other favorites

French Quarter

Strawberry Shortcake

3 cups sifted all-purpose flour

3$^{1/4}$ teaspoons double-acting baking powder

3 tablespoons sugar

1$^{1/4}$ teaspoon salt

1/2 cup shortening, softened

1 egg, well beaten

2/3 cup milk

3 pints (6 cups) strawberries, washed and hulled

Whipping cream

Sift flour, baking powder, sugar and salt into bowl. Cut in shortening. Add egg and enough milk to make a soft dough, mixing with fork. Knead lightly, about 20 turns on floured board. Divide in thirds. Pat out thirds in 3 greased 9" round cake pans. Bake at 450 degrees about 15 minutes. Divide berries in half and sweeten to taste. Put shortcake layers together with berries between and on top. Serve with whipped cream. Serves 6 to 8

New Orleans Pecan Pie

2 tablespoons shortening

1 cup brown sugar

2 tablespoons flour

1 cup light corn syrup

3/4 teaspoon salt

1 teaspoon vanilla

3 eggs, beaten

1 cup pecans, broken

Cream together shortening, sugar and flour. Add syrup and beat well. Add eggs, vanilla and salt and beat well again. Add pecans. Place in unbaked 9" pie shell for 15 minutes at 400 degrees, then 30 minutes at 325 degrees. Yields one 9" pie.

Bread Pudding with Whisky Sauce

Bread Pudding

3	cups bread cubes
4	cups hot milk
1/2	cup sugar
3	eggs, beaten
4	tablespoons margarine, melted
1/2	teaspoon salt
1	teaspoon vanilla
3/4	cup raisins
1/4	teaspoon nutmeg
1/4	teaspoon cinnamon

Add bread cubes to hot milk; set aside to cool. Add remaining ingredients. Pour into buttered pan. Place pan with pudding into larger pan of hot water. Bake for 1 hour at 350 degrees. Serve warm with Whisky Hard Sauce.

Whisky Hard Sauce

11/2	cup confectioners sugar
2	tablespoons butter, softened
1	tablespoon whisky

Stir together and let rest a few hours to blend flavors. If too thick, add a few drops of milk. Serve over bread pudding.

Almond Mocha Mousse

1/2	cup milk
4	ounces cream cheese, at room temperature
11/4	cups chocolate fudge topping
1/4	cup coffee liqueur
2	cups whipped cream
1/2	cup sliced almonds

Cream milk and cream cheese together. Add fudge topping and coffee liqueur and mix well. Whip cream until stiff enough to form peaks and fold gently into mousse. Pour equally into individual dessert bowls. Sprinkle with sliced almonds. Cover and chill in refrigerator until set. Serves 6

Fresh Fruit Tarts

Arrange fresh fruit, in season, such as strawberries, blueberries, kiwi, peaches or apricots over pastry cream in baked tart shells. Make glaze by warming apricot or peach preserves or red currant jelly and spreading over fruit.

Pastry Cream

4	cups milk
8	egg yolks
1	cup sugar
3/4	cup flour
2	tablespoons butter
1	teaspoon vanilla extract

Scald milk in a saucepan. In a mixing bowl, beat egg yolks with the sugar until the mixture is very thick and flows in a wide ribbon when the beater is withdrawn. Blend in the flour. Gradually pour in the heated milk, stirring constantly. Transfer the mixture to the saucepan and cook over medium heat. Continue to stir until all lumps are gone and sauce is thick and smooth. Blend in the butter and vanilla. Cool. Pour into pastry shell and chill. Remainder of cream may be stored in the refrigerator covered for 1 week or frozen for 1 month. Yields 4 cups cream.

Jackson Square

Tart or Pie Shell

1	cup unsifted all purpose flour
1/4	teaspoon salt
1	teaspoon sugar
1/3	cup vegetable shortening
3	tablespoons ice water

Put flour, salt and sugar in a bowl. Mix with fork. Add shortening; stir until mixture is crumbly. Gradually sprinkle in ice water, stirring lightly with fork until dry ingredients hold together. Form into a ball and wrap in waxed paper. Place in refrigerator for 20 minutes. Roll out on lightly floured surface. Fit into tart pans or pie pan. Bake in 450 degree oven for 12 to 15 minutes. Yields one 9" pie shell or 6 muffin-size tart shells.

Rum De La Creme

4	egg yolks
4	tablespoons sugar
3	egg whites, beaten stiff
1 1/2	cups whipped cream
1/2	cup rum

Beat egg yolks and sugar until thickened. Fold in egg whites and cream. Stir in rum and freeze about 8 hours. Serves 8.

White Coconut Cake with Lemon Filling

Baked Alaska

1	pound cake, sliced into layers
8	egg whites
1/8	teaspoon cream of tartar
1/2	cup sugar
1	teaspoon vanilla
1-2	pints vanilla ice cream

Place cake on oven proof platter. Form a mound with ice cream. Whip egg whites and cream of tartar until stiff then slowly fold in sugar and vanilla. Continue beating until very stiff. Completely cover cake and ice cream with meringue. Place in freezer. When ready to serve, set in a 450 degree oven and brown lightly for about 5 minutes. Serve immediately. Serves 8.

White Coconut Cake with Lemon Filling

1/2	cup butter
1/2	cup white shortening
2	cups sugar
11/2	cups buttermilk, divided
3	cups cake flour
1/2	teaspoon soda
1	teaspoon baking powder
1/2	teaspoon salt
1	teaspoon vanilla
4	egg whites, beaten stiffly

Cream shortening, butter, sugar and vanilla. Add 1/4 cup buttermilk and beat until fluffy. Add dry ingredients alternately with remaining buttermilk, beating to blend after each addition. Fold in beaten egg whites. Spread into three 9" cake pans. Bake at 350 degrees for 30 minutes or until done.

Lemon Filling

Grated rind of 1 lemon

1/2	cup sugar
1	teaspoon flour
1/4	cup lemon juice
1	egg, slightly beaten
1/4	cup cold water
1	teaspoon butter

Mix lemon rind, sugar and flour. Add lemon juice, egg, water and butter. Cook until thick, stirring constantly. Cool. Spread between cake layers.

Icing

3	cups granulated sugar
1	cup water
2	teaspoons vinegar
3	egg whites, beaten
1/2	teaspoon cream of tartar
1	teaspoon lemon extract
1	teaspoon vanilla extract
11/2	cups coconut, freshly grated

Stir together sugar, water and vinegar. Cook until it spins a fine hair-like thread. Beat egg whites with cream of tartar. Gradually add sugar mixture, beating constantly. Add lemon and vanilla extracts and mix well. Spread on cooled cake. Cover with coconut. Frosts tops and sides of two 9" cake layers.

Dessert Crepes

1	cup flour
1/8	teaspoon salt
1	tablespoon sugar
1	cup milk
1	egg, well beaten
2	tablespoon butter, melted

Mix the dry ingredients together and add the liquid ingredients. Beat until smooth. The batter should be the consistency of thin cream. Grease an 8" crepe pan or sauté pan lightly with butter and heat until butter is very hot but not burned. Pour or ladle about 1/3 cup of the batter into the pan and rotate the pan to spread the batter evenly. Cook the crepe until it looks firm and is slightly browned at the edges, about 1 minute, then turn over with a thin spatula and brown other side for about 30 seconds. Repeat until all batter is used, adding a little more butter as necessary. Stack the finished crepes and cover to prevent them from drying out. If desired, spread warmed apple sauce, sweetened strawberries, currant jelly or raspberry jam thinly on crepes and roll up. Sprinkle with sugar and serve. Yields 12 crepes.

Pound Cake

1	pound (2 cups) butter
1	pound (2-1/4 cups) sugar
9	eggs
4	cups sifted cake flour
1	tablespoon grated lemon rind
1	tablespoon lemon juice

Cream butter and sugar until very light and creamy. Beat in eggs, one at a time, beating well after each addition. Gradually add flour, blending thoroughly. Add lemon rind and juice. Bake in two greased, wax paper-lined 9" by 5" pans at 350 degrees for 1 hour and 15 minutes. Frost, glaze or leave plain. Slice thin to serve. Yields 2 loaf cakes.

Pound Cake with Berries

Pecan Pralines

Pecan Pralines

2   cups sugar
3/4   cup water
1/2   tablespoon vinegar
4   cups pecan halves

Put to boil sugar, water and vinegar until syrup makes a soft ball when dropped into cup of cold water. Put in pecans, cook until syrup forms a hard ball in cup of cold water. Have ready a large platter or pans greased with butter. Drop large spoonfuls of mixture about six inches apart, and let them cool. When hard and cold, run a knife under each praline and put on plate.

Bananas Foster
Brennan's

4   tablespoons butter
1/2   tablespoon cinnamon
4   bananas, cut in half lengthwise, then halved
1   cup brown sugar
4   tablespoons banana liqueur
4   scoops vanilla ice cream
1/4   cup rum

Melt the butter over an alcohol burner in a flambé pan or attractive skillet. Add the sugar, cinnamon and banana liqueur and stir to mix. Heat for a few minutes, then place the halved bananas in the sauce and sauté until soft. Add the rum and allow it to heat well, then tip the pan so that the flame from the burner causes the sauce to ignite. Allow the sauce to flame until it dies out, tipping the pan with a circular motion to prolong the flaming. Serve over vanilla ice cream. First, lift the bananas carefully out of the pan and place four pieces over each portion of ice cream. This is one of Brennan's most famous and most popular desserts. It's really quite simple to prepare. Wait until the rum gets hot, so that you get a good flame when it's ignited. This can also be prepared over a stove burner, then brought to the dinner table and flamed. Serves four.

Breakfast

French
Market
Beignets

Eggs
Sardou

Eggs
Benedict

French
Bread

And other
favorites

Beignets

New Orleans French Market Beignets

1   cup milk
2   tablespoons sugar
3/4   teaspoon salt
1/2   teaspoon nutmeg
1   envelope dry yeast
2   tablespoons lukewarm water
1   egg
2   tablespoons vegetable oil
31/2   cups sifted flour
   Fat for deep frying
   Sifted confectioners sugar

Scald milk and dissolve it in the sugar and salt. Add nutmeg. Let milk cool to lukewarm and combine with softened yeast in lukewarm water. Stir in the egg and oil and thoroughly blend in flour, a little at a time. Cover the bowl lightly with a cloth and let dough rise in a warm place until it has doubled in bulk, about 1-1/2 hours. Turn the dough out onto a well-floured pastry board, deflate it and knead it gently. Roll it out into a rectangle 18" long and 12" wide and cut it into 36 pieces, each 3" by 2". Cover lightly with a towel and let beignets rise on the pastry board for 30 minutes. In a fryer or large saucepan, heat fat for deep frying to 375 degrees. Cook the beignets, a few at a time, until they are golden brown. Drain them quickly. Dust immediately with confectioners sugar and serve at once while hot. Yields 36.

58

French Bread

1   package yeast
1/2   cup warm water for yeast
13/4   cup warm water for bread
2   tablespoons sugar
2   teaspoons salt
5-6   cups flour

Dissolve yeast in 1/2 cup warm water. Combine 1-3/4 cup water, sugar and salt. Cool to lukewarm. Stir in yeast mixture, mixing well. Add flour gradually; knead. Cover. Let rise until doubled in bulk. Punch dough down; let rise again. Shape into 2 loaves. Place on cookie sheet and let rise until doubled. Bake in 400 degree oven with a shallow pan of hot water on lower oven rack, about 45 minutes, until loaves are crusty and golden brown.

Brunch Egg Casserole

1   pound sausage, cooked and drained
4   large onions, diced
12   slices white bread, quartered
3   cups grated Cheddar cheese
8   eggs, beaten
4   cups milk
1/4   teaspoon pepper
1/2   teaspoon dry mustard

Sauté onion in sausage drippings until soft. Place 1/2 of the bread in the bottom of a greased 9 X 13 inch pan. Sprinkle 1/2 of sausage, onions and cheese on bread; repeat these layers. Combine eggs, milk and spices; pour over top layer. Refrigerate for at least 24 hours before cooking. Remove from refrigerator one hour before baking so that it allows casserole to come to room temperature. Bake at 350 degrees for 45 to 50 minutes. Serves 10.

Eggs Sardou

Creamed Spinach (recipe follows)
8   poached eggs
3/4 cup Hollandaise sauce
8   large artichoke bottoms, cooked

Creamed Spinach

4   cups spinach, chopped
1/2 cup butter
3/4 cup white onion, chopped
1/2 cup flour
2   cups milk
     Salt and pepper to taste

Melt butter over low heat in a heavy saucepan. Add the onion and cook until soft. Add the flour gradually, stirring constantly. Stir in the milk, a little at a time. Continue stirring and cooking until evenly blended and warmed through. Add the salt, pepper and spinach and cook a few minutes more, just until the spinach is warmed through and the mixture is evenly blended. Put equal amounts of the creamed spinach on 4 heated plates; place artichoke bottoms on top of spinach. Place 2 poached eggs side by side on each artichoke bottom, then ladle an even coating of Hollandaise sauce (page 39) over each portion. Serves 4.

Breakfast in the French Quarter

Eggs Benedict

6   slices toast or English Muffins, toasted
6   slices boiled ham *or* Canadian bacon
6   eggs
3/4 cup Hollandaise sauce
     Sprinkle of paprika

Place ham on toast and top with poached egg. Cover with Hollandaise sauce (page 39) and sprinkle with paprika. Serves 3 or 6.

Best Ever Biscuits

1/2 stick of butter, melted
4   ounces sour cream
2   cups biscuit baking mix
1/3 cup club soda

Preheat oven to 375 degrees. Melt butter in 9 inch pie pan, being careful not to let it burn. Mix sour cream and biscuit mix lightly and add club soda. Stir gently, with a rubber spatula, just enough to mix. Roll dough onto lightly floured board to 1/2 inch thickness. Cut with biscuit cutter and place into melted butter in pan. Bake until brown, about 12 minutes. Yields eight 2-1/2" by 1" biscuits.

Drinks

Irish
Coffee

Mint
Julep

Hurricane
Punch

Cyclone

And other
favorites

Hurricane Punch

Irish Coffee

Court of the Two Sisters

1   cup freshly brewed hot coffee
1   teaspoon sugar
11/2 ounce Irish whisky
1/4 cup whipped cream

Pour hot coffee into stemmed coffee glass or warmed mug. Add sugar and stir. Add Irish whisky and top with whipped cream. Serve with a straw.

Hurricane Punch

4   ounces dark rum
4   ounces Pat O'Brien's Hurricane Mix

Shake with cracked ice; strain into a chilled double cocktail glass. Garnish with an orange or lemon slice and a cherry.

Cyclone

2   ounces vodka
2   ounces Pat O'Brien's Gold Passion Fruit mix

Serve vodka and Passion Fruit Mix in a large brandy snifter with crushed ice and garnish with orange slice and cherry.

Grasshopper

3/4 ounce green Creme de Menthe
1/2 ounce white Creme de Cacao
3   tablespoons vanilla ice cream

Blend 30 seconds in blender. Pour carefully into champagne or cocktail glass.

Mint Julep

2   ounces bourbon
1   teaspoon simple syrup *or* 1 teaspoon sugar
4-5 fresh sprigs of mint

Crush mint with syrup in a small tumbler. Fill with crushed ice. Add bourbon and stir gently until glass is frosted. Garnish with an orange or lemon slice and more mint.

Screwdriver

11/2 ounces vodka
3   ounces orange juice

Shake with cracked ice. Strain into a chilled cocktail glass.

Pat O'Briens

Gin Smash

2	ounces gin
1	teaspoon simple syrup *or* 1 teaspoon sugar
6	mint leaves

Place syrup or sugar in a small tumbler; add mint and muddle (crush and mix). Add gin and fill with crushed ice. Garnish with mint sprig.

Shillelagh

2	ounces white rum
1	ounce green creme de menthe
1	ounce lime juice
	Green cherry

Serve in a large wine glass decorated with green straws, green cherry and green stick candy.

Ramos New Orleans Gin Fizz

1	tablespoon super fine sugar
1	egg white
	Juice of 1/2 lemon
1	dash vanilla
2	dashes Fleur d'Orange (orange flower water)
	or 1 teaspoon kirschwasser
2	ounces half and half (milk and cream)
11/2	ounces gin

Shake well with cracked ice. Strain into chilled goblet and fill with seltzer.

Mimosa

2	ounces orange juice, freshly squeezed
4	ounces domestic champagne

Serve in a wine glass with fresh strawberry.

Iced "Tea"

1/2 ounce gin
1/2 ounce vodka
1/2 ounce tequila
1/2 ounce rum
2 ounces Collins mix
1 ounce cola

Serve in a Zombie glass. Garnish with a long straw and fresh fruit on a skewer.

Smith and Kerns

3/4 ounce vodka
1/4 ounce Kahlua
3 ounces milk
1 ounce soda

Serve in Zombie glass.

Bloody Mary

11/4 ounces vodka
1/4 lime wedge
3 ounces tomato juice
3 dashes Worcestershire sauce
2 dashes salt
Dash of hot pepper sauce

Serve over ice in an Old Fashioned glass. Add celery stalk for stirrer.

Martini

11/2 ounces gin
3 drops dry Vermouth

Stir gently. Serve over ice or straight up in a cocktail glass with an olive.

Variations:

Gibson: Use a pearl onion instead of an olive.

Giblet: Use vodka instead of gin

Dry: Use no vermouth

Breeze Punch

11/2 ounce dark rum
1/2 ounce lemon juice
1/2 ounces Red Passion Fruit mix

Serve in a cocktail glass filled with crushed ice. Garnish with a twist of orange peel.

Strawberry Piña Colada

1 scoop French Vanilla ice cream
8 ounces cubed ice
1 ounce pineapple juice
1 ounce Coco Lopez (cream of coconut)
1/2 ounce cream
1 ounce rum
11/2 ounces strawberry cordial syrup
2 fresh strawberries for garnish
Pineapple slice for garnish

Crush ice in blender and add all ingredients except fresh strawberries. Garnish with strawberries and pineapple slice.

Variations:

Piña Colada: Substitute peach or banana cordial syrups and fresh peach and banana slices for garnish.

Mint Julep

Glossary

Andouille sausage:

Hot peppery, smoked pork sausage used in many Cajun dishes.

Beignets:

Fried, puffy rectangular doughnuts sprinkled with confectioners sugar. A New Orleans French Market specialty.

Blackened Fish:

Charred redfish, pompano, trout or other fish often done outside over a fire in a white hot cast iron skillet. To blacken indoors, heat skillet to the smoking point, dip fish in clarified butter, season, and cook a few minutes on each side.

Chicory:

A carrot-shaped root, dried, roasted and ground. Used as a seasoning for coffee.

Crawfish:

Fresh water shell fish resembling small lobsters.

Creole Trinity Sauce:

Green peppers, onions, celery; the three vegetables which form the basis for many Creole dishes from sauces to jambalayas and gumbos.

Crepe:

Thin, light pancake.

Filé:

Dried, ground sassafras leaves used to thicken gumbos.

Gumbo:

Neither a soup or stew, but a meal in itself, featuring meat, vegetables, herbs and a generous dash of hot pepper sauce, thickened with filé powder or okra, cooked slowly and served with cooked white rice.

Jambalaya:

A dish of ham, sausage, shrimp, spices, tomatoes and the Creole trinity traditionally incorporating rice into the cooking.

Roux:

A equal mixture of butter or other fat and flour blended and cooked slowly with liquid to act as a thickening agent for sauces and gravies.

Lump Crab Meat:

Flaked small pieces of white and dark meat from the blue crab body and claws.

Soft Shelled Crabs:

Crabs, usually blue crabs, during a few days' period when the old shell has shed and the new shell is soft and tissue thin.

Tasso:

Highly spiced, smoked ham. A Cajun specialty.